KITAAB ZONE

# 100 DIY Christmas Fun Ideas

## CREATE, CRAFT AND CELEBRATE THE HOLIDAY SEASON

# CONTENTS

# 1
# DECORATIONS AND CRAFTS

## 1.1

## Make Homemade Ornaments

Get creative and make your own personalized Christmas tree ornaments! Use materials like clay, felt, beads, buttons, paint, and more to design unique decorations.

## 1.2

## Create a Festive Wreath

Craft a beautiful Christmas wreath for your front door using fresh evergreen branches, pinecones, berries, and festive embellishments. Let your creativity shine!

# 1.3

## Design Personalized Stockings

Make each family member feel special by sewing or decorating unique Christmas stockings with their names or monograms. Add festive trim, buttons, ribbons, and more!

# 1.4

## Craft Paper Snowflakes

Cut intricate snowflake designs out of paper. Fold, cut, and decorate plain paper to create gorgeous wintry accents to hang around the house.

# 1.5

## Decorate a Gingerbread House

Have fun decorating a graham cracker or gingerbread house using frosting, candies, and treats. Get creative with your dream candy cottage!

# 1.6

## Make your own Christmas Cards

Design handmade Christmas cards using construction paper, markers, stickers, stamps, or photos. Personalize them for family and friends!

# 1.7

## Create a Centerpiece for the Table

Craft a beautiful Christmas centerpiece for your holiday dining table. Use pine branches, holly, candles, pinecones, ornaments, and ribbon.

# 1.8

## Paint Holiday-themed Rocks

Paint fun Christmas designs like snowmen, trees, stockings, or ornaments on smooth rocks to use as holiday decor.

# 1.9

## Craft a garland using popcorn or cranberries

Make a festive garland for your Christmas tree or mantel using popcorn, cranberries, paper chains, or beads threaded onto string.

# 1.10

## Make a DIY advent calendar

Design a unique countdown-to-Christmas advent calendar for kids using paper bags, socks, or homemade props. Fill with small treats!

# 2 FESTIVE TREATS AND RECIPES

## 2.1

### Bake and decorate sugar cookies

Make holiday memories by baking and decorating delicious sugar cookies cut into fun Christmas shapes. Decorate with frosting and sprinkles!

## 2.2

### Make hot chocolate with marshmallows

Warm up with rich and creamy homemade hot chocolate topped with marshmallows and your favorite fixings like whipped cream, cinnamon, or peppermint.

# 2.5

## Create a gingerbread cookie house

Have a tasty time decorating a gingerbread house with homemade or ready-made gingerbread cookies, royal icing, and loads of candy.

# 2.4

## Prepare a Christmas morning breakfast casserole

Make a hearty Christmas breakfast casserole ahead of time, with eggs, bread, sausage, veggies, and cheese. Just bake and serve on Christmas morning!

# 2.5

## Make candy cane-shaped treats

**Transform white chocolate bark or brownie batter into festive candy cane shapes. Crush up actual candy canes to decorate!**

# 2.6

## Create reindeer-shaped snacks

**Use pretzels, chocolate, and peanut butter to make Rudolph reindeer snacks for a fun Christmas treat.**

# 2.7

## Bake a Yule log cake

Make an impressive Yule log cake shaped and decorated like a miniature log with chocolate frosting, rosettes, and meringue mushrooms.

# 2.8

## Make homemade eggnog

Blend up classic eggnog at home with eggs, cream, sugar, nutmeg, and rum or bourbon for a decadent Christmas beverage.

## 2.9

# Prepare a holiday-themed charcuterie board

Arrange cured meats, cheeses, nuts, jams, fruit, and crackers on a board for a beautiful savory Christmas spread.

## 2.10

# Create a hot cocoa bar with various toppings

Create a hot cocoa bar with various toppings: Set up a hot cocoa bar with options like marshmallows, whipped cream, sprinkles, crushed candy canes, and flavored syrups.

# FAMILY TRADITIONS

## Watch a classic Christmas movie together

Snuggle up and bond as a family watching your favorite Christmas flick like A Christmas Story, Elf, or It's a Wonderful Life.

## Go ice skating as a family

Head to an outdoor rink and lace up your skates for some festive fun gliding around the ice together.

# 3.3

## Read Christmas stories aloud

Warm your heart reading favorite Christmas tales and poems like 'Twas the Night Before Christmas or A Christmas Carol.

# 3.4

## Have a family game night with holiday-themed games

Play festive board games, Christmas trivia, or video games together as a family. Enjoy hot cocoa and cookies!

## 5.5

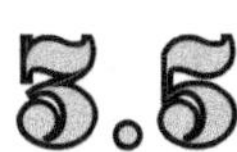

# Volunteer at a local charity or soup kitchen

Spread holiday cheer by spending time volunteering as a family at a charity, food bank, or soup kitchen.

## 5.6

# Decorate the Christmas tree together

Bond while decorating the Christmas tree with lights, garland, ornaments, tinsel, and the star on top. Play Christmas music!

# 5.7

## Write letters to Santa Claus

Keep the magic of Christmas alive by having kids write wish lists for Santa on Christmas Eve to leave out with milk and cookies..

# 5.8

## Attend a local Christmas parade or event

Get into the holiday spirit together at a local Christmas parade, tree lighting, concert, or winter festival.

# 5.9

## Have a family photo session in matching holiday outfits

Dress up in matching Christmas sweaters or outfits for an adorable family photo session to send out as holiday cards.

# 5.10

## Sing Christmas carols together

Spread Christmas cheer caroling with homemade songbooks or a Spotify carols playlist. Walk around your neighborhood or local nursing home.

# OUTDOOR ACTIVITIES

## Build a snowman

Make the most of a snow day by rolling massive snowballs and decorating your frosty snowman with carrots, scarves, and hats.

## 4.2

## Go sledding down a hill

Zip down snowy slopes together on toboggans, tubes, or sleds. Race to see who can get down the fastest!

# Have a snowball fight

Divide into teams and take cover behind snow forts for an epic snowball battle! Just remember to play nice.

# Go on a winter hike or nature walk

Explore the gorgeous icy wonderland on local trails. Look for animal tracks and enjoy the scenery.

## 4.5

# Decorate the exterior of your home with lights

**Deck out your home with dazzling Christmas lights, inflatables, wreaths, and holiday decorations.**

## 4.6

# Visit a local Christmas tree farm

**Hop on a hayride, sip hot cider, and cut down your own real Christmas tree at a festive local tree farm.**

#  4.7

## Take a horse-drawn carriage ride

**Snuggle under a blanket for a magical old-fashioned carriage ride to see the Christmas lights around town.**

#  4.8

## Go on a neighborhood Christmas lights tour

**Pile in the car with thermoses of cocoa to cruise around and admire the spectacular light displays.**

# 4.9

## Have a bonfire and roast marshmallows

**Make the most of a snow day by rolling massive snowballs and decorating your frosty snowman with carrots, scarves, and hats.**

# 4.10

## Go on a nighttime stargazing adventure

**Rug up warm and gaze at the clear winter night sky identifying constellations and shooting stars.**

# 5

# GIFT IDEAS AND EXCHANGES

## 5.1

## Secret Santa gift exchange

Have fun buying a thoughtful gift for a mystery person instead of stressing over buying for everyone.

## 5.2

## DIY personalized gifts

Make meaningful homemade gifts like photo books, baked goods, knitted scarves, and personalized art.

# 5.3

## Create a homemade coupon book for favors or experiences

Make a cute coupon book with free babysitting, dinners, massages, or handmade gifts you can redeem.

# 5.4

## Make a photo album or scrapbook for a loved one

Compile special photos and memories into a sentimental scrapbook or photo book gift.

# 5.5

## Homemade spa or bath products

Whip up pampering gifts like sugar scrubs, bath bombs, body butter, or soaps. Package them in jars or gift baskets.

# 5.6

## Create a custom playlist or mixtape

Make a personalized playlist gift by picking special songs that remind you of someone. Give it to them on a CD or flash drive. .

# 5.7

## Handmade jewelry or accessories

Make thoughtful gifts like earrings, bracelets, scarves, or headbands you designed. Choose meaningful beads, colors, or charms.

# 5.8

## Plan a surprise outing or experience

Give tickets for a fun excursion like a concert, play, mini golf, museum visit, or hiking adventure.

# 5.9

## Gift certificates for favorite restaurants or stores

Give the flexibility of gift cards for go-to food spots, coffee shops, retailers, spas, or entertainment.g for everyone.

# 5.10

## Write heartfelt letters to loved ones

Send touching handwritten notes expressing what loved ones mean to you. These letters can become treasured keepsakes.

# 6

# HOLIDAY GAMES AND ACTIVITIES

## 6.1

## Christmas trivia quiz

Test your holiday knowledge with a fun Christmas trivia game! Ask questions about movies, songs, traditions, Christmas history, and more.

## 6.2

## Scavenger hunt for hidden presents

Hide presents around the house and make clues leading to each one. See who can find all their gifts first!

# 6.3

## Play Christmas-themed charades

Act out classic Christmas movies, songs, characters, and traditions. See who can guess them right.

# 6.4

## Build a snow fort or igloo

Gather up mounds of snow to construct an epic snow fort or igloo. Decorate it with sticks, lights, and snow art.

# 6.5

## Have a wrapping paper fashion show

Craft inventive fashions from leftover wrapping paper, tape, ribbons and bows. Strut the runway to show them off!

# 6.6

## Play a holiday-themed board game

Have a holly jolly game night with Christmas versions of classic games like Monopoly, Jenga, Chess, Yahtzee, or Candyland.

# 6.7

## Put on a Christmas puppet show

Craft fun puppets and put on a creative Christmas play!
Use toys and props to make a whimsical performance.

# 6.8

## Have a snowflake cutting competition

Fold paper and carefully cut out intricate snowflake
designs. Compare and judge which are the most
creative and complex.

## 6.9

# Play "Pin the Nose on Rudolph"

Take turns being blindfolded and trying to pin
Rudolph's red nose in the right spot on his face.

## 6.10

# Create a holiday-themed puzzle
# to solve

Challenge yourself with a jigsaw puzzle featuring a fun
Christmas or winter picture to assemble.

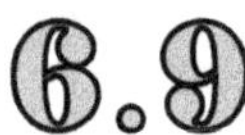

# DIY CHRISTMAS FASHION AND ACCESSORIES

## 7.1

### Make your own ugly Christmas sweater

Craft an intentionally tacky sweater decorated with pom poms, puff paint, tinsel fringe, and googly eyes.

## 7.2

### Design and create unique Christmas hats

Make Santa hats, elf hats with jingling bells, or wreath headbands using felt, sequins, and ribbons.

## 7.3

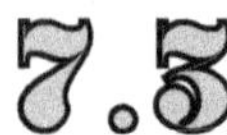

# Decorate Christmas-themed socks or stockings

Adorn plain socks with pom poms, buttons, puff paint, and other embellishments to make them festively fun.

## 7.4

# Craft a festive holiday brooch or pin

Design a Christmas brooch or pin with ribbon, beads, buttons, fabric scraps, or felt. Affix a pin back to wear it.

# 7.5

## Personalize Christmas-themed T-shirts or hoodies

CMake custom Christmas tees using iron-on designs, fabric paint, bleaching, stenciling, or sewing on patches.

# 7.6

## Create your own Christmas-themed jewelry

Make necklaces, bracelets, or earrings featuring beads, bells, candy canes, snowflakes, trees, or ornaments.

# 7.7

## Design and decorate Christmas-themed face masks

Craft sparkly, festive face masks embellished with ribbons, lace, rickrack trim, buttons, and appliqués.

# 7.8

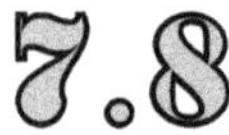

## Make DIY Christmas-themed hair accessories

Accent your holiday 'do with reindeer antler headbands or mini Christmas tree clips with felt bows.

# 7.9

## Customize Christmas-themed tote bags or backpacks

Decorate plain bags for carrying gifts using iron-on designs, puffy paint, sewing, or gluing on sequins and buttons.

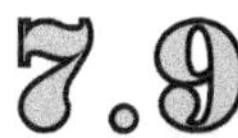

# 7.10

## Design and paint Christmas-themed shoes or sneakers

Make your kicks merry and bright by painting trees, snowflakes, candy canes, or Santa faces on them.

# 8

# DIY CHRISTMAS HOME DÉCOR

## 8.1

### Make a Christmas wreath for your front door

Craft a gorgeous holiday wreath using faux greenery, pinecones, berries, ribbon, and Christmas decorations.

## 8.2

### Create a Christmas-themed centerpiece for your dining table

Design a festive centerpiece with candles, pine branches, ornaments, pinecones, and other embellishments.

# 8.3 

## Design and make your own Christmas stockings

**Sew personalized stockings for each family member using felt, faux fur, and other cozy fabrics. Add names!**

# 8.4 

## Craft a unique Christmas tree skirt

**Sew or purchase a basic tree skirt, then decorate it with ribbon, fabric scraps, lace, beads, or appliqué.**

## 8.5

# Make a festive garland to hang around your home

**String together popcorn, paper chains, felt shapes, or cranberries to make a merry garland for trimming.**

## 8.6

# Create personalized Christmas candle holders

**Decoupage, mod podge, or paint candle jars or vases with holiday patterns, pictures, and designs.**

## 8.7

# Design and paint your own Christmas-themed wall art

Get creative painting canvas panels featuring holiday scenes, lyrics, or silhouettes to hang.

## 8.8

# Craft a Christmas-themed doormat

Adorn a basic coir mat with fabric, paint, or vinyl cutouts in Christmas colors and designs.

# 8.9

## Make your own Christmas-themed throw pillows

**Sew or hot glue fabric and trims on plain throw pillows to give them a festive holiday look.**

# 8.10

## Create a customized Christmas-themed photo frame

**Decorate standard frames with patterned scrapbook paper, washi tape, glitter, pine sprigs, and photos.**

# CHRISTMAS PARTY IDEAS

## 9.1

### Host a Christmas cookie exchange party

Have guests bring batches of homemade cookies to trade and sample everyone's recipes!

## 9.2

### Throw a Christmas movie marathon night

Snack on popcorn and goodies while watching a lineup of classic Christmas flicks.

# 9.3

## Organize a DIY Christmas ornament-making party

**Provide supplies like clay, beads, paint, and more for guests to make crafty ornaments.**

# 9.4

## Host a Christmas-themed costume party

**Ask guests to show up dressed as Santa, elves, reindeer and other festive characters. Have photo booth props.**

 9.5

# Plan a holiday-themed scavenger hunt

Hide clues leading to small prizes or treats all around the house or neighborhood for teams to locate.

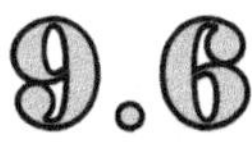 9.6

# Organize a festive Christmas karaoke party

Get the microphone going with a song list of holiday hits and classics. Dress in ugly sweaters!

# 9.7

## Throw a gingerbread house decorating party

Provide ready-to-assemble gingerbread kits, plenty of candy, and icing for sugary creations.

# 9.8

## Host a Christmas-themed trivia night

Test guests on their holiday movie, song, and tradition knowledge in lively trivia games.

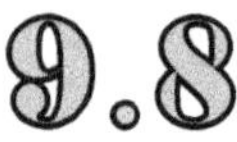

# 9.9 

## Plan a holiday-themed potluck dinner

Ask each guest to bring a favorite Christmas appetizer, entree, or dessert to share together.

# 9.10 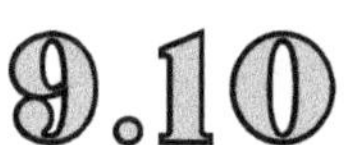

## Organize a Christmas book club meeting

Pick out a festive book to read, like A Christmas Carol, then meet up to discuss over snacks.

# 10
## ACTS OF KINDNESS AND GIVING BACK

## 10.1

### Volunteer at a local homeless shelter or food bank

Help out by donating your time to serve meals, sort donations, or spread cheer.

## 10.2

### Donate toys to a children's charity or hospital

Brighten a child's holiday by gifting new, unwrapped toys to organizations like Toys for Tots.

# 10.3

## Write letters or send care packages to military personnel

Express gratitude and provide comforts from home by mailing cards and care packages overseas.

# 10.4

## Collect donations for a local animal shelter

Help shelters care for animals in need by gathering pet food, blankets, toys, or other supplies to donate.

# 10.5

## Visit nursing homes and spend time with elderly residents

Spread joy during the lonely holidays by caroling, chatting, and engaging in activities with seniors.

# 10.6

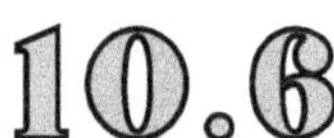

## Organize a fundraising event for a charitable cause

Host a fun run, craft fair, bake sale, or concert to raise money for a charity you care about.

# 10.7

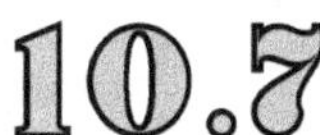

## Donate warm clothing to a homeless shelter

Clean out gently used coats, hats, gloves, and blankets to help keep those less fortunate warm.

# 10.8

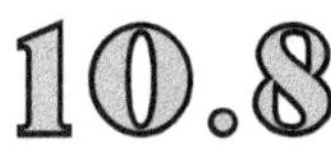

## Sponsor a family in need for the holidays

Provide gifts, meals, and support for a struggling family to brighten their Christmas.

# 10.9

## Participate in a charity run or walk for a good cause

Get active while fundraising by joining a 5K, fun run, or marathon benefiting charity.

# 10.10

## Spread kindness by performing random acts of kindness throughout the holiday season

Pay for someone's coffee, leave big tips, hand out gift cards, or help with groceries.

# 11
# CHRISTMAS-THEMED SCIENCE EXPERIMENTS

## 11.1

### Create a winter-themed sensory bin

Fill bins with fake snow, pinecones, pom poms, and forest critter figurines for tactile play.

## 11.2

### Make homemade snow or fake snow

Explore chemical reactions by mixing cornstarch and conditioner or baking soda and shaving cream to create "snow."

# 11.3

## Conduct a candy cane science experiment

**Observe how candy canes change and dissolve in different liquids like water, oil, and vinegar.**

# 11.4

## Explore the science behind Christmas lights

**Learn about conductors, insulators, and circuits by making a simple light up paper Christmas tree.**

# 11.5

## Grow a crystal Christmas tree

Make crystal tree shapes by suspending pipe cleaner "trees" in borax and water solutions.

# 11.6

## Experiment with melting ice and salt

See how salt lowers the freezing point of ice by melting ice cubes coated in salt. Time how fast they melt.

# 11.7

## Study the properties of hot chocolate and marshmallows

Investigate how cocoa particles and marshmallows respond to hot milk and how stirring affects dissolving.

# 11.8

## Create a homemade snow globe and learn about density

Explore density by creating snow globe ornaments using water, glitter or fake snow, and figurines.

# 11.9

## Investigate the chemistry of baking holiday treats

Learn chemistry concepts like leavening, caramelization, and emulsification that make baked goods possible.

# 11.10

## Explore the physics of sledding and friction

Conduct experiments with toy sleds on various surfaces to see how friction affects speed and motion.